To Max,
Celtic won the
league again
on 22/5/08
lots of love
Auntie Gwen
xxx

The Official
Celtic Football Club Annual 2008

Written By Joe Sullivan & Gregor Kyle

Special thanks to Thomas Quinn
for all his great ideas.

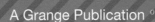

A Grange Publication

© 2007. Published by Grange Communications Ltd., Edinburgh,
under licence from Celtic Football Club. Printed in the EU.

Every effort has been made to ensure the accuracy of information
within this publication but the publishers cannot be held
responsible for any errors or omissions. Views expressed are
those of the author and do not necessarily represent those of the
publishers or the football club. All rights reserved.

Photographs by Alan Whyte & Angus Johnston
Celtic logo is a registered trademark of The Celtic Football Club.
ISBN 978-1-905426-80-5

£6.99

Contents

CLUB HONOURS

SCOTTISH LEAGUE WINNERS [41 TIMES]

1892/93	1893/94	1895/96	1897/98
1904/05	1905/06	1906/07	1907/08
1908/09	1909/10	1913/14	1914/15
1915/16	1916/17	1918/19	1921/22
1925/26	1935/36	1937/38	1953/54
1965/66	1966/67	1967/68	1968/69
1969/70	1970/71	1971/72	1972/73
1973/74	1976/77	1978/79	1980/81
1981/82	1985/86	1987/88	1997/98
2000/01	2001/02	2003/04	2005/06
2006/07			

SCOTTISH CUP WINNERS [34 TIMES]

1892	1899	1900	1904
1907	1908	1911	1912
1914	1923	1925	1927
1931	1933	1937	1951
1954	1965	1967	1969
1971	1972	1974	1975
1977	1980	1985	1988
1989	1995	2001	2004
2005	2007		

LEAGUE CUP WINNERS [13 TIMES]

1956/57	1957/58	1965/66	1966/67
1967/68	1968/69	1969/70	1974/75
1982/83	1997/98	1999/00	2000/01
2005/06			

EUROPEAN CUP WINNERS 1967

CORONATION CUP WINNERS 1953

CLUB DIRECTORY & HONOURS

Celtic Football Club
Celtic Park, Glasgow,
G40 3RE

Telephone:
0871 226 1888

Website:
www.celticfc.net

Formed:
1888

Stadium:
Celtic Park

Capacity:
60,456

Home strip colours:
Green/white hooped shirts,
white shorts, white socks

Away strip colours:
Black Forest Green
with silver trim

Record attendance:
92,000 v Rangers, 1938

Record victory:
11-0 v Dundee, 1895

Record defeat:
0-8 v Motherwell, 1937

**Most league goals
in one season:**
50 - Jimmy McGrory,
1935/36

**Most Premier/SPL
goals in one season:**
35 - Brian McClair, 1986/87
35 - Henrik Larsson, 2000/01

CLUB SPONSORS

Celtic plc Directors:
Brian Quinn
Peter Lawwell
Eric Riley
Dermot Desmond
Tom Allison
Brian McBride
Brian Wilson

CFAC Directors:
Peter Lawwell
Eric Riley
John Keane
Michael McDonald
Kevin Sweeney

Manager:
Gordon Strachan

Assistant Manager:
Garry Pendrey

Coach
Tommy Burns

Head of Youth:
Tommy Burns

**Football
Development Manager:**
John Park

Reserve Coach:
Willlie McStay

Youth team Coach:
John McLaughlan

Club Doctor:
Derek McCormack

Physiotherapists:
Tim Williamson &
Gavin McCarthy

Kit Controller:
John Clark

Celtic's Clydesdale Bank Premier League Fixtures

All fixtures subject to change.

DATE	TEAM
05/08/07	Kilmarnock (H)
11/08/07	Falkirk (A)
19/08/07	Aberdeen (A)
25/08/07	Hearts (H)
02/09/07	St Mirren (A)
15/09/07	Inverness CT (H)
23/09/07	Hibernian (A)
29/09/07	Dundee United (H)
07/10/07	Gretna (A)
20/10/07	Rangers (A)
27/10/07	Motherwell (H)
03/11/07	Kilmarnock (A)
10/11/07	Falkirk (H)
24/11/07	Aberdeen (H)
01/12/07	Hearts (A)
08/12/07	St Mirren (H)
15/12/07	Inverness CT (A)
23/12/07	Hibernian (H)
26/12/07	Dundee United (A)
29/12/07	Gretna (H)
02/01/08	Rangers (H)
05/01/08	Motherwell (A)
19/01/08	Kilmarnock (H)
26/01/08	Falkirk (A)
09/02/08	Aberdeen (A)
16/02/08	Hearts (H)
23/02/08	St Mirren (A)
27/02/08	Inverness CT (H)
01/03/08	Hibernian (A)
15/03/08	Dundee United (H)
22/03/08	Gretna (A)
29/03/08	Rangers (A)
05/04/08	Motherwell (H)

Gordon Strachan

TWO seasons, four trophies and the club's first steps into the latter stages of the Champions League have made Gordon Strachan one of Celtic's most successful modern-day managers.

The club's domestic success has also earned him a raft of personal accolades, most notably the Manager of the Year Award two years in a row.

This success has only increased his desire for a job that he describes as one of "the biggest and most exciting in world football."

Several new faces arrived at Celtic Park in the summer of 2006, and the Champions began the defence of their title in impressive style, quickly building up a commanding lead at the top of the table.

Dutch internationalist Jan Vennegoor of Hesselink arrived from PSV Eindhoven to become a firm fan favourite while Shunsuke Nakamura carried on from the previous season, his form throughout the season resulting in a clean-sweep of Scotland's Player of the Year Awards.

Having booked their place in the last 16 of the Champions League with memorable wins over Manchester United, FC Copenhagen and Benfica, the Hoops were finally knocked out of the competition by eventual winners, AC Milan, in extra-time.

Meanwhile, Celtic continued to dominate on the domestic front, winning the SPL title by an impressive 12-point margin and lifting the Scottish Cup at Hampden in May. In just two seasons Gordon Strachan has won every domestic prize on offer, but you can bet that he will have his eye on more silverware in season 2007/08.

Factfile:

D.O.B: 09/02/57

Born: Edinburgh, Scotland

Playing career record: Dundee (1974-77), Aberdeen (1977-84), Manchester United (1984-89), Leeds United (1989-95), Coventry City (1995-97)

Playing honours: Scottish Championship 1980, 1984 / Scottish Cup 1982, 1983, 1984 / UEFA Cup-Winners' Cup 1983 / UEFA Super Cup 1983 / English FA Cup 1985 /, English Second Division (old) 1990, English First Division (Old) 1992, FA Charity Shield 1992

Managerial history: Coventry City (1996-2001), Southampton (2001-2004), Celtic (2005-present)

Managerial honours: Scottish Premierleague Championship 2005/06, 2006/07 / Scottish League Cup 2005/06 / Scottish Cup 2006/07

50 Scotland caps and member of the SFA Hall of Fame
Scottish Football Writers' Player of the Year 1980
English Football Writers' Player of the Year 1991
Scottish Football Writers' Manager of the Year 2006 & 2007
Scottish PFA Manager of the Year 2007
FIFA/SOS Ambassador for Scotland

SEASON REVIEW
2006/07

JULY/ AUGUST

CELTIC unfurled the league flag before their opening game of the season against Kilmarnock and then proceeded to put on a display fit for champions, destroying the visitors 4-1 with Jiri Jarosik nabbing his first goal for the club.

Unfortunately, that was followed up by a 2-1 defeat at Tynecastle against Hearts, though it was to prove to be Celtic's only league defeat until the following March.

Gordon Strachan's side got immediately back to winning ways in their third league game of the season, winning 2-0 at home to St Mirren, though two further points were dropped when the Hoops travelled to Inverness.

August finished with a 2-1 victory over Hibernian at Celtic Park, when Jan Vennegoor of Hesselink came off the bench to score his first goal for the club and the winner on the day.

The result left Celtic at the top of the SPL table, ahead on goal difference from Hearts.

"It's great to be top. We've got the same points as last year (after five games) but we're in a better position than we were last season, because Hearts were five points ahead of us at this stage."

Gordon Strachan after the Hibs game

SEPTEMBER

JAN Vennegoor of Hesselink confirmed his importance to the team when he scored his second consecutive goal to give Celtic a 1-0 victory over Aberdeen at Pittodrie. The match also saw Thomas Gravesen make an impressive debut for the club.

Four days later and it was the start of the Champions League group stages. Gordon Strachan's side had the toughest of starts – facing Manchester United at Old Trafford – and Vennegoor of Hesselink put the Hoops ahead with a brilliant first-half goal.

Despite a valiant effort though, Celtic lost out 3-2 in a night of drama. However, later in the month they would record their first victory in that season's competition, beating FC Copenhagen 1-0 courtesy of a Kenny Miller penalty to reinforce the image of Celtic Park as a European fortress.

League wins over Dunfermline and Rangers, which included Kenny Miller's first Celtic goal, consolidated the Champions' position at the top of the table, where they now enjoyed a three-point lead over Hearts.

"We are playing in the Champions League to win, so we will be aiming for the best result possible in every game. It doesn't matter who we are playing against, whether it's Manchester United, Copenhagen or Benfica – home or away, we should still be aiming to beat them."

Artur Boruc after the Old Trafford game

SPL Player of the Month ALLAN McGREGOR (Rangers)

OCTOBER

CELTIC'S victory over Falkirk courtesy of an Aiden McGeady strike showed once again that Gordon Strachan's side were able to come back from the European exertions and still dominate domestically.

Shunsuke Nakamura then provided a one-man demolition job of Dundee United at Tannadice, netting a hat-trick in the 4-1 victory.

And that was followed up with the demolition of Benfica at Celtic Park as Strachan's men produced one of the best European performances ever seen at Paradise.

Kenny Miller led the way with two goals, while Stephen Pearson put the icing on the cake, and supporters began to believe that this could be the season for progress in the Champions League.

Two consecutive 2-1 victories – over Motherwell and Kilmarnock respectively – pushed Celtic's lead at the top of the SPL to 10 points and already it looked as though the league trophy would be remaining at Celtic Park.

"The 3-0 win over Benfica was massive for us. It was a brilliant performance from the whole team and the goals were pleasing. For the first goal, I missed my chance after Lee (Naylor) crossed, but Kenny Miller managed to get his foot to the ball and put it on target. The second and third goals were excellent."

Shunsuke Nakamura after the Benfica game

SPL Player of the Month LEE NAYLOR (Celtic)

"When the penalty was given I got that sick feeling in the pit of my stomach. But as Louis Saha was getting ready to take the kick, Gary Neville came over to me and said, 'His head has gone - I think he's going to miss this!' Artur made a brilliant save and he'd made another just before when Saha thought he was offside. He realised he wasn't and tried to scoop it over Artur and that was probably when his head started to go."

Neil Lennon on Artur Boruc's penalty save v Man United

NOVEMBER proved to be a busy month, with Celtic facing seven games in three different competitions. It also provided some European highs and lows.

The month started badly for the Hoops as they lost 3-0 to Benfica in Lisbon, though towards the end of November there was another memorable Champions League night at Celtic Park when Shunsuke Nakamura's wonderful free-kick just nine minutes from time gave Celtic a 1-0 victory over Manchester United, helped in no small measure by a last-minute Artur Boruc penalty save.

Results elsewhere meant further celebration on the night as Gordon Strachan's side qualified for the last 16 of the competition for the first time.

In the league, the Hoops remained dominant, beating Hearts thanks to a late Craig Gordon own goal and also rescuing a point against Hibernian at Easter Road after going two goals down. Their lead at the end of November was now 13 points.

However, the CIS Cup holders were knocked out of that competition after a penalty shoot-out by Falkirk.

NOVEMBER

SPL Player
of the Month
RUSSELL
ANDERSON
(Aberdeen)

DECEMBER

A NARROW 1-0 victory over Aberdeen thanks to a Maciej Zurawski goal was followed by another disappointing away result in Europe as FC Copenhagen won 3-1 in Denmark.

However, the draw for the last 16 of the Champions League was made during December and Celtic knew they were facing a tough task, up against AC Milan.

The Hoops remained unbeaten in the league throughout December, which included a 1-1 draw at Ibrox when Thomas Gravesen was on target for the second consecutive derby game.

Celtic also required the sublime skill of Shunsuke Nakamura when Dundee United were the visitors to Celtic Park on Boxing Day.

Trailing 2-0, Darren O'Dea pulled a goal back for the Hoops before Nakamura's incredible chip from the edge of the box levelled the score. The goal was later voted the best of the season by the SPFA.

Celtic's lead at the top of the table going into 2007 was now 17 points.

"The calendar year has been fantastic for us. It was disappointing to lose to Clyde early in the year but we've gone a long way to repairing that damage by winning the CIS Cup, winning the league and getting through to the last 16 of the Champions League. I hope all the supporters have enjoyed the past year and it would be good if 2007 was similar. I'm sure obstacles will be in our way, but we have to be ready for them."

Gordon Strachan looking back on a whirlwind 12 months

SPL Player of the Month Artur Boruc (Celtic)

JANUARY

THE New Year began with a new face at Celtic Park in the shape of Steven Pressley. The former Hearts captain joined the Champions and made his debut in the 2-0 home victory over Kilmarnock.

A third-round Scottish Cup tie against Dumbarton was comfortably negotiated before Celtic grabbed another dramatic win over Hearts, winning 2-1 thanks to a goal from Jiri Jarosik.

Jan Vennegoor of Hesselink hit a hat-trick as St Mirren were beaten 5-1 at Celtic Park. It was

"It was the club in general that swayed me – Celtic sells itself. It's a club of great tradition, a fantastic football club. It's a perfect move and one that really excites me. I think that's vitally important in football - you need to be excited by the environment you're playing in. My heart was telling me to come here."

Steven Pressley on his move to Paradise

the second hat-trick against the Paisley side, with Thomas Gravesen scoring all three back in November at Love Street.

And Celtic finished off January with a 2-1 away victory over Inverness Caley Thistle. Goals from Derek Riordan and a last-minute Jan Vennegoor of Hesselink strike gave Gordon Strachan's side all three points, although the big Dutchman received a second yellow card and his marching orders for his celebrations.

SPL Player of the Month JAN VENNEGOOR OF HESSELINK (Celtic)

FEBRUARY

CELTIC began and ended February with victories in the Scottish Cup.

At the beginning of the month, it was a comfortable 4-1 victory over Livingston, which included two Derek Riordan goals, though the last game in February proved a lot closer.

Indeed, it looked as though Celtic were on their way out of the competition as they trailed Inverness Caley Thistle 1-0. But goals from Steven Pressley and a dramatic injury-time winner from Kenny Miller put the Hoops into the semi-final of the competition.

"We have to believe we're good enough to go there and get a result. Defensively we did very well but there weren't any of us at our best when we were attacking. We know we can play better, so it's too early to say we can't get past AC Milan. We still have a big, big chance to get through. I believe 0-0 is not a bad scoreline. It is going to be a top match in the San Siro because that is one of the great places to play football anywhere in the world. I have been there before and it is fantastic."

Shunsuke Nakamura after the 0-0 draw with AC Milan

The first leg of Celtic's Champions League last 16 tie against AC Milan took place in Glasgow, and Gordon Strachan's side recorded a creditable 0-0 draw with the Italian giants.

And in the league, victories over Hibernian and Aberdeen saw Celtic march inexorably towards a second consecutive league title, their lead now an incredible 19 points ahead of Rangers in second place.

MARCH

WHILE March began with a 2-1 victory over Dunfermline, the month was to prove the toughest of the campaign for Gordon Strachan's side.

Heartache followed in the Champions League when the Hoops went out of the competition, losing 1-0 in the San Siro after extra-time.

In 180 minutes of football, AC Milan had not managed to score against Celtic, for whom Stephen McManus and Darren O'Dea were heroic in the heart of the defence.

But with Celtic also failing to hit the net, it took an extra-time effort from Kaka to separate the sides.

Celtic also lost for the first time in the SPL since August, and it was a 1-0 home defeat against Rangers, which was followed up by another 1-0 defeat, this time away to Falkirk.

And a last-minute strike by Dundee United gave them a share of the spoils at Tannadice when it looked as though the Hoops were going to leave with all three points thanks to a Shunsuke Nakamura free-kick.

"We can take a few things from the week, making chances all over the place, playing well against Milan and coming out with a rather sickly feeling, but we have to deal with that. I think we have handled everything brilliantly, I didn't think we were unfit and I thought that at the end of the 120 minutes we were still running and chasing everything against Milan."

Gordon Strachan following the extra-time defeat against AC Milan

SPL Player of the Month
ALAN HUTTON
(Rangers)

BANK OF SCOTLAND
PREMIERLEAGUE CHAMPIONS 2006 - 2007

BANK OF SCOTLAND
PREMIERLEAGUE
CHAMPIONS 2006-2007

BANK OF SCOTLAND PREMIERLEAGUE

BANK OF SCOTLAND PREMIERLEAGUE

CELTIC remained on course for a league and cup double with a 2-1 semi-final victory over St Johnstone at Hampden.

And on April 22 at Rugby Park, Shunsuke Nakamura crowned an impressive season with an injury-time free-kick that sealed the title for Celtic.

It was a second consecutive title for Gordon Strachan's side who had once again dominated the domestic scene.

And for player and manager, the plaudits continued to roll in.

Nakamura was voted Players' Player of the Year and Football Writers' Player of the Year, while his equaliser against Dundee United at Celtic Park on Boxing Day was voted Goal of the Season.

And Gordon Strachan also scooped the Manager of the Year Award from both of the aforementioned organisations.

A defeat at home to Hearts couldn't take the shine off the title celebrations as the trophy was presented to captain Neil Lennon.

The Irishman lifted the trophy for the last time as a Celtic player, having announced he would be leaving the club at the end of the season.

"I saw the movement of the goalkeeper at the previous free kick. So this time I knew he would move to the near post, which is why I sent the shot to the far post. It was a tough game for us. Celtic always have to win their games, but there was extra pressure on us for this. It has been a good season, playing well in the Champions League and we've won the league again. Now our aim is to win the Scottish Cup."

Shunsuke Nakamura following his title-clinching goal

SPL Player of the Month
NEIL LENNON
(Celtic)

MAY

SPL Player of the Year SHUNSUKE NAKAMURA (Celtic)

THE three league games played in the early stages of the month were never going to take top billing during May although the Celts finished off their home campaign with a 2-1 win over Aberdeen.

And then there was the strange spectacle of Celtic fans cheering a goal against their own club when Scott Brown signed off with Hibernian by scoring against his soon-to-be new club.

However, the real focus was on the final game of the season – the Scottish Cup final - as supporters everywhere hoped to finish the season on high with a Double AND say farewell to the departing Neil Lennon as he played his final game for the Celts.

As it turned out, the skipper did finish his seven-year Celtic career by lifting his eleventh winner's medal as the Bhoys lifted the oldest trophy in world football for the 34th time thanks to a Jean-Joel Perrier-Doumbe goal five minutes from time.

"It's a day of celebration and we've finished the season as double winners. The boys have made a wee bit of history for themselves and for the history of the club. I couldn't ask for any more and it's a great way for me to finish my career here. I just wish the club and the fans all the success in the world. I hope they get as much enjoyment out of being involved with Celtic as I did."

Neil Lennon at Hampden after lifting the Scottish Cup

There are twelve differences in this double take of Evander Sno, the first one has been done, see if you can spot the rest.

SPL SEASON 2006/07 CHAMPIONSHIP QUIZ

Stephen McManus celebrates a 'goal' but he wasn't credited on the scoresheet (See question 12).

QUESTIONS:

01 Who was Celtic's top scorer in the SPL campaign?

02 Which Celt scored the goal that finally clinched the SPL title?

03 And at which ground was that goal scored?

04 Which young Celt made his debut in the final league game of the season?

05 What was Celtic's final points tally for last season?

06 Which goalkeeper made his Celtic debut during the season?

07 Celtic's highest-scoring game was against which side?

08 And which Celt scored a hat-trick in that game?

09 Who were the visitors to Celtic Park when the Championship trophy was presented?

10 What was the score in Celtic's first SPL game of the season?

11 How many players appeared for Celtic in the SPL for the first time during the season?

12 How many of Celtic's 65 goals were OGs by the opposition?

(Answers on Pages 60/61)

Did you know...
That the theme for The Celtic Song comes from Gilbert and Sullivan's comic opera, The Pirates of Penzance?

DEAD-BALL DELIVERY
...with Shunsuke Nakamura

SHUNSUKE NAKAMURA SAYS:

"When I was a kid I had to practice how I hit the ball, because I was very skinny and didn't have any muscles in my legs, so I wasn't able to curl the ball or put any real power in my shots.

So when I would get home from school each day I would stand with the ball in front of a wall and try and kick the ball at the same spot, over and over again.

Then, once I started to improve my accuracy and build up my muscles, I would still try and hit the same spot on the wall, but this time using different parts of my foot, such as the outside of my foot – which allows me to curl my shots.

Nowadays there are so many good keepers out there that when I hit a free-kick, I have to think about getting the ball up and over the wall and back down and on target as quickly as I can.

When you curl a shot, the ball moves slower, so once you practise curling the ball and hitting the one spot, you have to try and work on doing that with as much power as possible.

TRAINING TIPS

- To strike the ball with force, in a straight line, use your laces to strike the ball and ensure that your standing foot leaves the ground on impact for greater power.
- To swerve the ball, use your toes and your instep to kick around the ball.

TRAINING EXERCISES

Stand in front of a wall or a goal with the ball in front of you and place your standing foot next to the ball.

Your standing foot should point towards where you want the ball to go and you should put your arms out to balance.

Strike the ball but swing through with your leg after you have struck the ball.

Once you are comfortable striking the ball, you can put a jumper over the top corner of the goal and use it as a target. Try and hit the jumper with the ball to improve your accuracy.

But you shouldn't become disheartened if it takes you time to hit that one spot in the wall. You will do it eventually and I used to keep hitting the ball until my leg was too sore to continue! Sometimes you see very talented players who don't have to practice as often. But if you are like me and don't have that talent, you have to keep practicing and one day you will become better than the talented player."

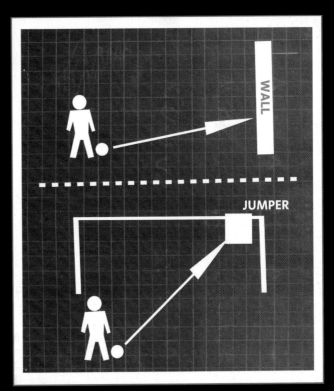

CONTACT CELTIC IN THE COMMUNITY

For more information, or to book any Celtic in the Community course throughout Scotland:
Call the Hotline: 0871 226 1888 (Option 5)
Telephone: 0141 551 4321

PARADISE PARADE

CELTIC PARK has a long and illustrious history. The first ground, just around the corner from the current one, was opened on May 8, 1888 and the club moved to the present site in 1892. Various modernisations were made over the years but in season 1994/95, three quarters of the ground was flattened and the magnificent Celtic Park we know and love today rose from the rubble. Here are just some of Paradise particulars.

Turf Accounting

Working on an average of 30 blades of grass per square inch, there are over 332million blades of grass on the playing surface alone which is 93% sand. Those 332million blades of grass are mown up to 150 times per year to keep the hallowed turf in tip-top condition The dimensions of the playing surface are 105m x 68m and over 26 miles of undersoil heating pipes run below the turf.

Safety First

For the biggest games there can be up to 600 police on duty, with 200 of those inside the stadium working with 718 stewards as well as 47 St Andrew's medical staff and 25 Fire Stewards.

From Hot Dogs to À La Carte

Up to 50 Celtic chefs in nine kitchens are among the 500 staff who cater for the nutritional needs of the support on a matchday.
There are 46 catering outlets in the stadium and in the three restaurants, 11 boxes, eight lounges and five suites, up to 3,300 supporters are catered for.

The Slopes of Celtic Park

There are 60,456 seats in the stadium and 150 of these are for wheelchair users and carer seats, while the Blind Party section accommodates 50 who receive their own commentary via earphones and a special sound system attached to their seats.

Stadium Stats

- There are 400 phone lines within Celtic Park and up to 300 computer workstations.
- The concourses within the stadium contain 85 plasma TVs.
- Over 6,000 tonnes of steelwork was used in construction – the highest amount in stadia at that time.
- The pitch is lit by 204 Phillips Arenavision 1,800-watt lamps producing an average Lux level of 1,700lms.
- The 20 square metres, nine-tonne Big Screens were the largest in the UK when they were installed and can be lowered to the ground for maintenance.
- The height of the stadium is 34 metres.
- The Kerrydale Suite perimeter wall can be opened to allow access for large display conference items such as cars.
- There are 80 toilets situated within the stadium.
- There are eight lifts inside Celtic Park.

Media Mayhem

On a Champions League night there can be as many as 200 press men watching the match, along with 120 TV personnel, 30 radio crew and 60 photographers clicking away on the sidelines, as well as 18 TV cameras positioned around the pitch taking in the action to be beamed worldwide.

Who Ate All The Pies

On a big matchday at Celtic Park around 20,000 pies and 2,000 portions of chips are sold as well as the 600 meals in the restaurants.
They are washed down with 10,000 pints in one of the 13 bars or the 7,000 soft drinks and 5,000 hot drinks poured in the 46 catering outlets.

Can you help Scott Brown find his way from Celtic Park to
the Lennoxtown Training Complex through this maze?
Find out how Scott got there on Pages 60/61.

WORDSEARCH

See if you can find the 10 Celtic words contained within the grid from the clues below. The words can appear horizontally, vertically or diagonally.

W	E	B	M	S	H	M	F	P	Q	O	G	L	E	S
V	L	I	A	L	C	Z	U	I	E	P	A	K	M	S
T	V	B	G	R	E	T	N	A	Y	G	U	O	S	E
E	I	I	A	J	M	L	V	R	U	D	T	Z	E	N
X	S	I	L	R	A	T	X	T	U	H	H	L	I	R
W	F	E	W	B	R	C	R	I	E	S	O	Y	K	E
E	Q	J	L	M	X	O	Y	R	J	U	O	T	C	V
I	I	N	B	H	P	T	W	S	G	V	P	D	X	N
V	H	T	R	E	Q	E	N	F	J	H	Y	R	E	I
C	B	N	M	J	L	E	Y	B	I	R	D	E	W	S
I	I	N	H	L	D	J	C	Z	S	E	W	Q	A	R
T	V	B	Y	P	J	H	A	I	O	P	L	M	K	J
L	R	E	M	U	I	B	V	P	D	F	C	D	S	W
E	D	A	C	I	T	N	H	J	A	P	D	F	C	X
C	H	I	U	O	T	M	C	A	R	N	Y	I	T	O

CLUES:

01 Before Lennoxtown, Celtic trained here.
02 The country where Celtic's Lions roared.
03 Celtic's four-legged friend.
04 Where the Scottish Cup was won.
05 The outlook from the club's magazine
06 Steven Pressley's nickname.
07 Scott McDonald's former club.
08 Celtic played against this club for the first time this year.
09 The country Shunsuke Nakamura hails from.
10 Where Celtic scored a dramatic last-minute winner in last season's Scottish Cup quarter-final.
(Answers on Pages 60/61)

QUESTIONS:

01 Celtic won the double in 2006/07 but which Celt lifted the League Cup during the same season?
02 Who did Celtic play in the semi-final of the Scottish Cup?
03 Shunsuke Nakamura's goal against which side ensured Celtic were through to the last 16 of the Champions league?
04 Which Celt moved on in the summer after more than 300 games for Celtic?
05 And how many goals did he score in those 300 games?
(Answers on Pages 60/61)

QUIZ:

Did you know…
That because of the route the River Clyde takes through Glasgow, Celtic Park is actually further south than Ibrox?

PARADISE PROFILES

Celtic Squad — 8 ♦
Gary Caldwell

Celtic Squad — 4 ♣
Lee Naylor

Celtic Squad — 9 ♦
Artur Boruc

Gary Caldwell
Position: Centre-back
Squad Number: 5
D.O.B: 12/04/82
Born: Stirling, Scotland
Height: 5'11"
Signed: 01/06/06
Debut: v Kilmarnock (h)
4-1 (SPL) 29/07/06
Previous Clubs:
Derby County (loan),
Coventry City (loan),
Darlington (loan),
Newcastle United,
Hibernian

Lee Naylor
Position: Left-back
Squad Number: 3
D.O.B: 19/03/1980
Born: Walsall, England
Height: 5'10"
Signed: 25/08/06
Debut: v Hibernian (h)
2-1 (SPL) 26/08/06
Previous Clubs:
Wolverhampton
Wanderers

Artur Boruc
Position: Goalkeeper
Squad Number: 1
D.O.B: 20/02/1980
Born: Siedlce, Poland
Height: 6'4"
Signed: 14/07/05 (loan)
17/10/05 (signed)
Debut: v Artmedia Bratislava
(h) 4-0 (UCL) 02/08/05
Previous Clubs:
Legia Warsaw,
Pogon Siedlce,
Dolcan Zabki (loan)

Bobo Balde
Position: Centre-back
Squad Number: 6
D.O.B: 05/10/75
Born: Marseille, France
Height: 6'3"
Signed: 21/07/01
Debut: v Dunfermline (h)
3-1 (SPL) 08/09/01
Previous Clubs:
Marseilles,
Toulouse

Maciej Zurawski
Position: Centre-forward
Squad Number: 7
D.O.B: 12/09/76
Born: Poznan, Poland
Height: 5'11"
Signed: 20/07/05
Debut: v Artmedia Bratislava (a)
5-0 (UCL) 27/07/05
Previous Clubs:
Lech Poznan,
Wisla Krakow

Mark Brown
Position: Goalkeeper
Squad Number: 21
D.O.B: 28/02/81
Born: Motherwell, Scotland
Height: 6'1"
Signed: January, 2007
Debut: v Hibernian (a)
2-1 (SPL) 20/05/07
Previous Clubs:
Rangers,
Motherwell,
Inverness Caledonian
Thistle

2 ♥ Celtic Squad
Bobo Balde

K ♦ Celtic Squad
Maciej Zurawski

6 ♥ Celtic Squad
Mark Brown

Jan Vennegoor of Hesselink
Position: Centre-forward
Squad Number: 10
D.O.B: 07/11/78
Born: Oldenzaal, Netherlands
Height: 6'3"
Signed: 25/08/06
Debut: v Hibernian (h)
2-1 (SPL) 26/08/06
Previous Clubs:
FC Twente,
PSV Eindhoven

Kenny Miller
Position: Centre-forward
Squad Number: 9
D.O.B: 23/12/79
Born: Edinburgh, Scotland
Height: 5'10"
Signed: 01/07/06
Debut: v Kilmarnock (h)
4-1 (SPL) 29/07/06
Previous Clubs:
Hibernian,
Stenhousemuir (loan),
Rangers,
Wolverhampton
Wanderers

K ♠ Celtic Squad K ♠

Jan Vennegoor
of Hesselink

K ♣ Celtic Squad K ♣

Kenny Miller

Celtic Squad

Q ♣ — Mark Wilson

K ♥ — Derek Riordan

Q ♣ — Paul Hartley

Derek Riordan
Position: Forward
Squad Number: 14
D.O.B: 16/01/83
Born: Edinburgh, Scotland
Height: 5'10"
Signed: 23/06/06
Debut: v Kilmarnock (h)
4-1 (SPL) 29/07/06
Previous Clubs:
Hibernian

Mark Wilson
Position: Full-back
Squad Number: 12
D.O.B: 05/06/84
Born: Glasgow, Scotland
Height: 5'10"
Signed: 16/01/06
Debut: v Dundee United (h)
3-3 (SPL) 28/01/06
Previous Clubs:
Dundee United

Paul Hartley
Position: Midfielder
Squad Number: 11
D.O.B: 19/10/76
Born: Glasgow, Scotland
Height: 5'8"
Signed: 31/01/07
Debut: v Livingston (a)
4-1 (SC) 04/02/07
Previous Clubs:
Hamilton,
Millwall,
Raith Rovers,
Hibernian,
St Johnstone, Hearts

Celtic Squad 8 ♥

Jiri Jarosik

Celtic Squad 7 ♠

Steven Pressley

Celtic Squad 5 ♦

Evander Sno

Jiri Jarosik
Position: Midfielder
Squad Number: 20
D.O.B: 27/10/77
Born: Usti nad Labem, Czech Republic
Height: 6'4"
Signed: 19/06/06
Debut: v Kilmarnock (h) 4-1 (SPL) 29/07/06
Previous Clubs: Sparta Prague, Slovan Liberec, CSKA Moscow, Chelsea, Birmingham (loan)

Steven Pressley
Position: Centre-back
Squad Number: 17
D.O.B: 11/10/73
Born: Elgin, Scotland
Height: 6'
Signed: 29/12/06
Debut: v Kilmarnock (h) 2-0 (SPL) 02/01/07
Previous Clubs: Rangers, Coventry City, Dundee United, Hearts

Evander Sno
Position: Centre-midfield
Squad Number: 15
D.O.B: 09/04/87
Born: Dordrecht, Netherlands
Height: 6'1"
Signed: 21/06/06
Debut: v Kilmarnock (h) 4-1 (SPL) 29/07/06
Previous Clubs: Ajax, Feyenoord, NAC Breda

Thomas Gravesen
Position: Midfielder
Squad Number: 16
D.O.B: 11/03/76
Born: Vejle, Denmark
Height: 5'10"
Signed: 30/08/06
Debut: v Aberdeen (a) 0-1 (SPL) 09/09/06
Previous Clubs: Vejle, Hamburger SV, Everton, Real Madrid

Darren O'Dea
Position: Defender
Squad Number: 48
D.O.B: 04/02/87
Born: Dublin, Ireland
Height: 6'1"
Signed: 01/08/2005
Debut: v St Mirren (h) 2-0 (SLC) 19/09/06
Previous Clubs: Celtic Youth

9 ♣ Celtic Squad
Thomas Gravesen

4 ♠ Celtic Squad
Darren O'Dea

John Kennedy
Position: Centre-back
Squad Number: 41
D.O.B: 18/08/83
Born: Bellshill, Scotland
Height: 6'2"
Signed: 20/08/99
Debut: v Motherwell
(h) 4-0 (SPL) 05/04/2000
Previous Clubs:
Celtic Youth

Cillian Sheridan
Position: Centre-forward
Squad Number: 26
D.O.B: 23/02/89
Born: Cavan, Ireland
Height: 6'2"
Signed: 10/02/06
Celtic Debut: v Inverness(a)
1-2 (SC) 25/02/07
Previous Clubs:
Celtic Youth

10 ♠ Celtic Squad 10 ♠

John Kennedy

3 ♠ Celtic Squad 3 ♠

Cillian Sheridan

Celtic Squad

Aiden McGeady

Celtic Squad

Stephen McManus

Celtic Squad

Shunsuke Nakamura

Aiden McGeady
Position: Midfielder
Squad Number: 46
D.O.B: 04/04/86
Born: Glasgow, Scotland
Height: 5'10"
Signed: 20/07/02
Debut: v Hearts
(a) 1-1 (SPL) 25/04/04
Previous Clubs:
Celtic Youth

Stephen McManus
Position: Centre-back
Squad Number: 44
D.O.B: 10/09/82
Born: Lanark, Scotland
Height: 6'2"
Signed: 20/08/99
Debut: v Hibernian
(a) 0-4 (SPL) 21/03/04
Previous Clubs:
Celtic Youth

Shunsuke Nakamura
Position: Midfielder
Squad Number: 25
D.O.B: 24/06/78
Born: Kanagawa, Japan
Height: 5'10"
Signed: 29/07/05
Debut: v Dundee United (h)
2-0 (SPL) 06/08/05
Previous Clubs:
Yokohama Marinos,
Reggina

Scott Brown

Position: Midfielder

Squad Number: 8

D.O.B: 25/06/85

Born: Hill o' Beath, Scotland

Height: 5'10"

Signed: 01/07/07

Debut: N/A

Previous Clubs: Hibernian

8 ♠
Celtic Squad

Scott Brown

8 ♠

Chris Killen

Position: Striker

Squad Number: 33

D.O.B: 08/10/81

Born: Wellington, New Zealand

Height: 6'

Signed: 02/06/07

Celtic Debut: N/A

Previous Clubs: Man City, Wrexham (loan), Port Vale (loan), Oldham, Hibernian

3 ♥
Celtic Squad

Chris Killen

3 ♥

Scott McDonald

Position: Centre-forward

Squad Number: 27

D.O.B: 21/08/83

Born: Melbourne, Australia

Height: 5'8"

Signed: 01/07/07

Debut: N/A

Previous Clubs:
Motherwell,
Milton Keynes Dons (loan),
Bournemouth (loan),
Huddersfield (loan),
Southampton

3 ♦ Celtic Squad 3

Scott McDonald

Massimo Donati

Position: Midfielder

Squad Number: 18

D.O.B: 20/02/1980

Born: Sedegliano, Italy

Height: 6'1"

Signed: June, 2007

Debut: N/A

Previous Clubs: Atalanta,
AC Milan,
Parma (loan),
Torino (loan),
Sampdoria (loan),
Messina (loan)

10 ♣ Celtic Squad 10

Massimo Donati

TRICKS OF THE TRADE
...with Aiden McGeady

AIDEN McGEADY SAYS:

"When I was growing up I was out practicing with a ball every single day and everybody says that practice makes perfect - but you need to want to get out there and practice every day by yourself.

As you are practicing, you will find yourself becoming more and more comfortable with the ball and better at what you are doing so you will be able to take those different skills into games with you.

But motivation is vital and I think if you want to make it to the top, it's important that you get out there and practice off your own back. You can't rely on other people to tell you to do it.

There are different exercises that you can do, but I was always just out playing with a ball every day and if you do that, you get more and more used to it, more comfortable when you are on the ball and you become a better player overall.

It's slightly different if you're playing for a team, because you are playing every week and training regularly and your coach may give you a few things that you can work on at home.

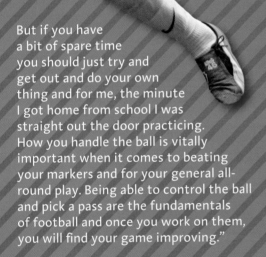

CELTIC in the COMMUNITY

TRAINING TIPS

- Take lots of small touches on the ball to make sure it stays nice and close to your body.
- Try and keep your head up when you're dribbling to make sure you can see where you're going.
- Practice dribbling with both of your feet to ensure you are as comfortable with one as you are with the other.
- Use different parts of your feet, such as the inside and outside of your boot, to change direction and turn.
- Once you are better at dribbling in a straight line, try turning and changing direction with the ball.
- It's really important to keep the ball close at all times to make sure a defender can't take it from you.

TRAINING EXERCISES

Try playing 1 v 1 with a friend. Set up two very small goals facing each other and try to dribble past your friend and through the goals to score points.

If you are practicing on your own, set up a starting cone, and another six cones in a 'slalom' as shown.

Using both feet, dribble in and out the cones and back.

Use different surfaces of your feet when controlling the ball, such as the inside and outside of your boot and use the sole of your foot to drag the ball across your body.

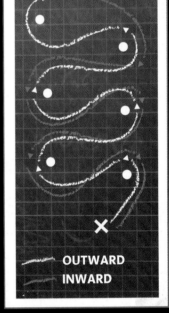

OUTWARD
INWARD

But if you have a bit of spare time you should just try and get out and do your own thing and for me, the minute I got home from school I was straight out the door practicing. How you handle the ball is vitally important when it comes to beating your markers and for your general all-round play. Being able to control the ball and pick a pass are the fundamentals of football and once you work on them, you will find your game improving."

CONTACT CELTIC IN THE COMMUNITY

For more information, or to book any Celtic in the Community course throughout Scotland:
Call the Hotline: 0871 226 1888 (Option 5)
Telephone: 0141 551 4321

CELTIC is a worldwide institution, with supporters in every corner of the globe. And the current Hoops stars have also come from far and wide to play football in Scotland. Here we have a look at their homelands and find out some facts that are strange but true.

ICELAND (Teddy Bjarnason)
Capital: Reykjavik   Currency: Icelandic Krona
Population: 301,931   2006/07 champions: FH Hafnarfjördur
Did you know: That Iceland is home to the oldest parliament in the world – the Althing - which was founded in 930 AD. But it has no army or military defence force.

SCOTLAND (Mark Brown, Scott Brown, Gary Caldwell, Paul Hartley, John Kennedy, Stephen McManus, Kenny Miller, Steven Pressley, Derek Riordan and Mark Wilson)
Capital: Edinburgh
Currency: Pound Sterling
Population: 5,000,000
2006/07 champions: Celtic
Did you know: Scotland may be one of the world's smallest countries, but it is also one of the most innovative, with Scots inventing telephones, television, refrigeration, penicillin and more recently the world's first cloned mammal!

IRELAND (Aiden McGeady, Darren O'Dea & Cillian Sheridan)
Capital: Dublin   Currency: Euro
Population: 4,109,086
2006/07 champions: Shelbourne
Did you know: That a grand total of nine people turned up to U2's first gig at the Dandelion Market in Dublin. They went on to become the world's biggest band in 2001, earning £32million.

ENGLAND (Lee Naylor)
Capital: London   Currency: Pound Sterling
Population: 50,690,000
2006/07 champions: Manchester United
Did you know: That the Bank of England was actually founded by a Scotsman, William Paterson, in 1694.

GUINEA (Bobo Balde)
Capital: Conakry   Currency: Guinean Franc   Population: 9,947,814
2006/07 champions: Fello Star
Did you know: Guinea is known as West Africa's "water reservoir" with the Fouta Djalon mountain range the source of hundreds of rivers.

THE NETHERLANDS (Evander Sno & Jan Vennegoor of Hesselink)
Capital: Amsterdam   Currency: Euro   Population: 16,570,613
2006/07 champions: PSV Eindhoven
Did you know: That about half of Holland is less than one metre above sea level, with one third of the country actually below it. The water is kept in check by a series of dams.

WORLDWIDE HOOPS

DENMARK (Thomas Gravesen)
Capital: Copenhagen   Currency: Danish Krone
Population: 5,468,120
2006/07 champions: FC Copenhagen
Did you know: That the Danish toy-makers, Lego, are also the world's biggest tyre manufacturers, making over 306million miniature tyres every year.

JAPAN (Shunsuke Nakamura)
Capital: Tokyo   Currency: Yen
Population: 127,433,494
2006/07 Champions: Urawa Red Diamonds
Did you know: Japan is made up of over 3,000 islands, four of which account for 97% of the land area. Many of those islands are volcanic and the nation's highest peak, Mount Fuji, is also an active volcano.

POLAND (Artur Boruc & Maciej Zurawski)
Capital: Warsaw   Currency: Zloty
Population: 38,518,241
2006/07 champions: Zaglebie Lubin
Did you know: According to Polish folk belief, it is unlucky to marry in a month whose name does not contain the letter 'R'. In Polish, according to their spelling, the unlucky months are January, February, April, May, July and November.

NEW ZEALAND (Chris Killen)
Capital: Wellington
Currency: New Zealand Dollar
Population: 4,115,771
2006/07 champions: Auckland City FC
Did you know: That at one time sheep outnumbered humans 20 to one in New Zealand. But today, with the country's woolly population shrinking, there are 12 sheep for every one person.

CZECH REPUBLIC (Jiri Jarosik)
Capital: Prague   Currency: Czech Koruna
Population: 10,228,744
2006/07 champions: Sparta Prague
Did you know: That the Latin name for the Czech Republic (Bohemia) comes from the name of the Celtic tribe that first settled in the area in pre-Roman times.

AUSTRALIA (Scott McDonald)
Capital: Canberra   Currency: Australian Dollar
Population: 20,434,176
2006/07 champions: Melbourne Victory
Did you know: Australia may be known for its koalas and kangaroos, but it is also an insect heaven, with over 1,500 different species of spiders and over 6,000 different types of flies.

ITALY (Massimo Donati)
Capital: Rome   Currency: Euro
Population: 58,147,733
2006/07 league champions: Inter Milan
Did you know: That in Italy the number 13 is omitted from the national lottery draw for superstitious reasons.

A SHIRT FIT FOR HEROES

The Celtic Annual has a sneak inside look at NIKE's launch of Celtic's current strip

CELTIC launched their new Nike home kit for season 2007/08 just before the Scottish Cup final victory and the traditional Hoops shirt honours the 40th anniversary of the club's European Cup triumph.

The visual design of the new kit reflects the uncomplicated hoops design of that era, with a simple round-neck in white trim on the shirt, white shorts with green trim and plain white socks. However, it is the detailing on the kit which evokes memories of the Lisbon triumph.

The club crest on both the shirt and shorts has a gold star unique to European Cup winners above it, with the words '25 MAIO 1967 – LEÕES DE LISBOA – 40° ANIVERSARIO' around it in gold.

On the bottom hem of the shirt, a small patch commemorates the famous moment in the tunnel before the game, where, as the teams lined up ready to come out, the Celtic team began to sing the club's anthem (to the consternation and confusion of their Italian opponents).

The patch reads 'For it's a grand old team to play for' The Tunnel. Estádio Nacional. 25th May 1967.

On the back neck of the shirt, above the player's name and number area is a design with CELTIC 1967 and the word LISBON under a gold star. A similar motif is also found on the calf area of the socks.

On the inside of the shirt on the neckline, a tape

carries the words: --1967--The Lisbon Lions 40th Anniversary--2007--.

The kit uses Nike Sphere Dry fabric technology, first used by Nike in national team kits worn by Nike-sponsored teams in the 2006 World Cup. This technology is designed to enhance player performance by wicking sweat through the material and away from the skin.

The fabric has a three-dimensional design with raised nodes on the underside that lift it away from the players' bodies to reduce 'cling' and allow air to circulate, assisting the body's own natural evaporation process. Mesh inserts on the side of the shirt also aid ventilation.

THE ART OF GOALKEEPING
...with Artur Boruc

ARTUR BORUC SAYS:

"To be a good goalkeeper, you first of all need to be hard-working and secondly, you need a little bit of luck in life.

For me I have always been really happy in life. I don't care about mistakes or dwell on the past. I always try to look forward and for a young goalkeeper this is very important.

Being a goalkeeper is one of the most under-appreciated jobs in football and you can save everything during a game and then in the last minute make a mistake that costs the team and you are the villain. But you cannot think about that.

You also have to work hard, listen to your coaches and of course, you have to really enjoy what you are doing.

To practice you can do exactly the same things as you would do when you are training as an outfield player.

When you are out in the street you can hit a ball against a wall, using both feet and then catch it. This improves your handling and I still do that now, after training I'll sometimes stand in front of a wall and just try to improve my handling.

You can also work on your natural fitness and your movement when you are doing this by diving to get the ball.

If you work hard, when it comes to a game, it will all just come naturally and you will be able to react without thinking, but I even dream about games and making saves at night.

There have been at least three occasions, once when I was asleep on a plane, when I have suddenly dived and been woken by my wife shaking me and asking what I am doing.

Even when I am watching games on television I dive when there is a shot on goal. People look at me like I am crazy, but when you are a goalkeeper, this is what happens!"

TRAINING TIPS

- Catch the ball low, with one knee on the ground when the shot is coming along the ground.

- Keep your elbows in and 'pinkie fingers' together to catch the ball in your 'basket' if the shot is coming in around your waist.

- Put your thumbs together and spread your fingers to make a 'W' shape when the shot is around your chest or above.

TRAINING EXERCISES

Stand facing a wall, five big steps away. Practice throwing the ball with one hand against the wall 12 times. The first four times make sure the ball rebounds along the floor.

Give yourself five points for every time you collect the ball properly down low with one knee on the ground.

Then, for the next four times throw the ball at the wall so it rebounds towards your waist. Give yourself five points for every time you collect the ball properly – without dropping it - as in tip No.2.

Then, for the next four times throw the ball at the wall so it rebounds above your chest. Give yourself five points for every time you save the ball properly – without dropping it - as in tip No.3.

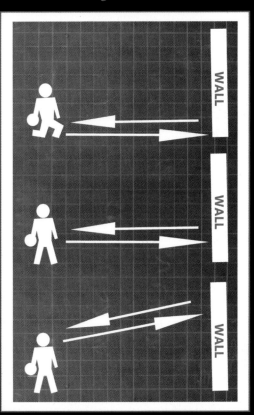

CONTACT CELTIC IN THE COMMUNITY

For more information, or to book any Celtic in the Community course throughout Scotland:
Call the Hotline: 0871 226 1888 (Option 5)
Telephone: 0141 551 4321

COLOUR ME IN

Shunsuke Nakamura is on the prowl against AC Milan here and we want you to get out your crayons, ink markers or paints and bring this empty image to full Celtic technicolour.

GUESS WHO?

1

2

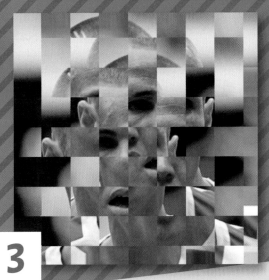

3

4

5

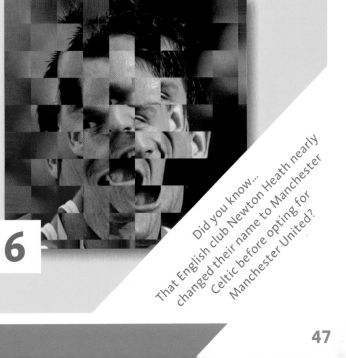

6

Did you know...
That English club Newton Heath nearly changed their name to Manchester Celtic before opting for Manchester United?

ALPHABET HOOP

A is for 'Annual'
This is the 18th edition of the Celtic Annual, which was launched in 1991 with Charlie Nicholas, Martin Hayes and John Collins as the first cover Bhoys.

B is for 'Bhoys'
The oldest and best-known nickname for both the team and the supporters stems from the club's Irish roots and remains popular to this day.

C is for 'Captain'
Neil Lennon, Jock Stein, Kenny Dalglish, Danny McGrain, Roy Aitken and Paul McStay have all worn the armband with distinction, while Billy McNeill is Celtic's greatest captain – winning seven Scottish Cups, six League Cups, nine championships and one European Cup.

D is for 'Drama'
Few gave Celtic a chance of winning the league when they travelled through to Love Street on the final day of the season in 1986. But with title-favourites Hearts losing 2-0 to Dundee and Celtic hammering St Mirren 5-0, the championship was clinched on goal difference in the most dramatic fashion.

E is for 'Evergreen'
Several Celts have spent their entire playing careers at Celtic Park, most notably the legendary Billy McNeill and 'the Maestro' Paul McStay.

F is for 'Four-leaf Clover'
The badge of Celtic Football Club first appeared on club literature in the early 1890s and was incorporated into the Celtic strip in 1977.

G is for 'Goalscorers'
The legendary Jimmy McGrory is Celtic's top scorer with an incredible 472 goals in 445 appearances. Lisbon Lion Bobby Lennox is in second-place with 273, with Henrik Larsson in third with 242.

H is for 'Hampden'
The National Stadium has witnessed many memorable Celtic victories including many of the 34 Scottish Cup and 13 League Cup wins - the most famous of which was a 7-1 win over Rangers in 1957!

I is for 'India'
Abdul Salim is the only Indian to have pulled on the Hoops, appearing as a trialist in reserve games during the 1936/37 season. The striker is remembered for wearing bandages on his feet instead of football boots!

J is for 'Jinky'
The 'Greatest Ever Celt' as voted by the supporters, Jimmy 'Jinky' Johnstone won the European Cup and nine consecutive league titles during 14 years as a Celtic player.

K is for 'King'
There have been two players crowned 'King' during their time at Celtic Park, 'King' Kenny Dalglish in the 1970s and more recently, Henrik 'King of Kings' Larsson.

L is for 'Lisbon'
The club's finest hour, where the Lisbon Lions won the 1967 European Cup with a 2-1 victory over the mighty Inter Milan.

M is for 'Managers'
A total of 16 men have managed Celtic since the club's founding days, with Willie Maley taking the reins for the first time in 1897 and Gordon Strachan, the current manager, taking over in 2005.

N is for 'Nine-in-a-row'
With their nine back-to-back title wins between 1966 and 1974, Jock Stein's Celtic set a new record in Scottish football history

It's as easy as ABC and here we have a concise look at Celtic from A to Z.

O is for 'Old Bhoys'
Alec 'The Icicle' McNair is the oldest player to have pulled on the Hoops, aged 41 years and 4 months in 1925. Next in line is Ronnie Simpson who played his last game aged 39 in 1969.

P is for 'Paradise'
The earliest nickname given to Celtic Park when the then-new stadium was first built on the present site back in 1892.

Q is for 'Quality Street Kids'
The name (taken from a popular brand of chocolates) which was given to the group of young Celts, including Lou Macari, Kenny Dalglish, Paul Wilson, George Connelly and Danny McGrain, that emerged from the youth team in the late '60s.

R is for 'Record breakers'
Celtic have played in two of the best attended games in European history, the Scottish Cup final against Aberdeen in 1938 which was watched by 146,433 and the European Cup semi-final, attendance 136,505, against Leeds in 1970 which set a UEFA record.

S is for 'Seville'
One of the biggest days in Celtic's recent history with over 80,000 supporters travelling to Spain on May 21, 2003 to see the team lose 3-2 to Porto after extra-time in the UEFA Cup final.

T is for 'Transfers'
Scott Brown's transfer from Hibernian to Celtic was the biggest between two Scottish clubs. But the fees have increased dramatically since the 1940s, when Celtic paid their first five-figure sum (of £12,000) to Clyde for Leslie Johnston and even the late 1970s, when Celtic paid a club record £120,000 for Davie Provan.

U is for 'Uruguay'
The scene of one of the club's most infamous matches, where Celtic were defeated in their third and final meeting with Argentina's Racing Club for the World Club Championship. Six players were sent off in a game that was marred by Racing Club's tactics.

V is for 'the V Factor'
Every one of Celtic's opponents en route to the UEFA Cup Final defeat in 2003 featured the letter 'V' in their name and where was the final held that season…. Seville!

W is for 'Walfrid'
The religious name of Andrew Kearns, the Irish Marist Brother who founded Celtic Football Club as a means of raising funds for the poor in the East End of Glasgow. His statue stands at the entrance to Celtic Park.

X is for 'X-Rated'
If the match in Uruguay has gone down in infamy, so too has Celtic's 'X-rated' meeting with Atletico Madrid in April 1974. Six Spanish players were suspended for the second leg of this meeting, where Celtic, and Jimmy Johnstone in particular, were kicked out of the European Cup.

Y is for 'Young Bhoy'
Mark Fotheringham is the youngest player to pull on the Hoops for a competitive match, making his SPL debut in a 0-0 away draw with St Johnstone in May 2000, aged 16 years, six months and 21 days.

Z is for 'Zurich'
Celtic's first opponents in the 1966/67 European Cup-winning run. The Lisbon Lions also beat Nantes, Vojvodina and Dukla Prague en-route to the final against Inter Milan.

USING YOUR HEAD
...with Stephen McManus

STEPHEN McMANUS SAYS:

"The most important thing for any young player is to listen closely to their coaches and manager and try and take on every piece of advice and information that they are given.

The coaches have more experience than you, they can see weaknesses in your game that are

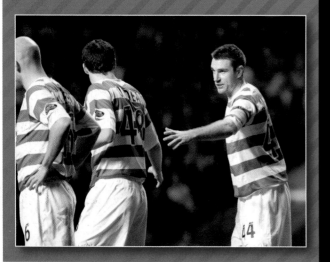

impossible for you to notice while you are playing and they'll have your best interests at heart.

It's important to always try and learn during games and training and it's particularly important to learn from your mistakes, rather than dwell on them and let them affect your confidence.

There are a lot of different aspects to your game that you can work on as a defender and your strength and physical fitness is certainly one of them. When you are young, you are still growing and getting stronger, but eating the right food and getting plenty of rest before and after games will help you a lot.

You should also work on your game after school and try and improve on any weaknesses you have, for example by working with both feet and improving your general control of the ball.

Then, during matches, you should always communicate with your fellow defenders and your goalkeeper and be careful not to be rash in your challenges.

When you are making tackles and winning headers, timing is everything."

TRAINING TIPS

- When heading the ball, keep your eyes open and on the ball at all times.
- Header the ball with your forehead.
- Raise your arms to help you balance.
- Try and 'take-off' using one leg.
- For a defensive header – head through the ball to send it high and long.
- For an attacking header – head more to the top of the ball to steer it down into the corner of the goal.

TRAINING EXERCISES

Hold a soft ball in your hands, two yards away from a ball on a marker. Using an 'attacking header' technique throw the ball in the air and try and header your ball down to hit the other ball off the marker.

Once you start improving, throw your ball higher in the air and try jumping to head the ball down. Move further away from the ball on the marker.

Then, using a 'defending header' technique throw your ball in the air and try to put as much power and height on the header as you can.

Remember to keep your eyes open and head the ball using your forehead, right through the ball.

Once you start improving, throw your ball off the wall, jump in the air and time your header to have as much power and height as you can.

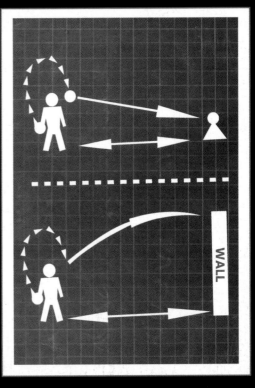

CONTACT CELTIC IN THE COMMUNITY

For more information, or to book any Celtic in the Community course throughout Scotland: Call the Hotline: 0871 226 1888 (Option 5) Telephone: 0141 551 4321

CelticONE

CelticONE JUNIORS

The unique Celtic fan club with a special section for Junior Members
Glasgow Celtic is football's unique family. The CelticONE membership gives you the
opportunity to be more than just a fan, you are part of the bigger family.
Not only are you part of our future you'll get ALL the following benefits as part of
your 2007/08 CelticONE Membership.

News

Keep up to date with what the team are up to and other members in a number of
ways. This year we have introduced a dedicated website for CelticONE Members at
www.celticfc.net. In addition you will receive regular updates from Hoopy by e-mail.
For those members too busy to look on the internet Hoopy will bring you up to
date in his CelticONE pages featured every week in the Celtic View available every
Wednesday – a must for all CelticONE Members. Hoopy has also confirmed he will
send three newsletters to his Junior CelticONE members in the season.

Competitions

Hoopy loves competitions and he will have regular prize draws throughout the
season, CelticONE members can win match tickets, exclusive signed shirts and the
latest Celtic merchandise. The Hoopy pages in the Celtic View will feature regular
competitions, open to all with some amazing and unique prizes for the winners.
You have to be in it to win it and you can also win places at the CelticONE Junior
Christmas Party.

Mascot

For a day never to be forgotten, you can line up with your heroes and Hoopy. The
matchday mascot is randomly selected from our Junior membership, you will meet
the team - have your photos taken and walk out with the team on to the magnificent
Celtic Park and experience the famous Celtic welcome, you will be the envy of all your
friends, not forgetting your uncles too.

Celtic View

The club magazine has your own pages - competitions, CelticONE member news
updates and the CelticONE member fanfile. Also there are the birthday files and if it's
your birthday Hoopy will have it printed so you can show friends and family.

Birthday & Christmas Card

You will receive a special card to celebrate your birthday and at Christmas your
favourite card will be from Celtic.

Membership Pack

All members will receive a unique souvenir pack and a personal Club Membership Card which is also your Celtic Teamcard.

PLUS

5% discount In the Club Shop on all merchandise excluding Nike products and sale items.
10% discount on dining at the Number 7 Restaurant on Friday Nights (booked In advance and excluding special events).
15% discount on any Celtic in the Community Course.
And discounts on holidays when booked directly with Thomas Cook Holidays.

I am waiting to hear from you. I want us to work as a team, AS ONE, as CelticONE. So as well as entering great competitions, I want you to send in your fanfile profiles and photos of your visits to Celtic Park, meeting your favourite players or even wearing your Celtic tops on holiday and I'll do my best to get them published in Hoopy's Gallery. You can send your photos to me at CelticONE Membership, Ticket Services, Celtic Park, Glasgow G40 3RE. Enclose a stamped addressed envelope if you want your pictures returned.

You can always email me on celticone@celticfc.co.uk

I can't wait to hear from you!

HOOPY

DOT TO DOT

Join up all the dots in this picture and see if you can identify the Celtic star about to take part in the Scottish Cup final victory over Dunfermline last season.
(Answer on Pages 60/61)

★ Indicates new line start.

SCOTTISH CUP FINAL
26th MAY 2007

25 MALO 1967
THE CELTIC FOOTBALL CLUB
LISBOA - 40TH ANIVERSARIO
LEÕES DE LISBOA
1888

CARLING

EUROPEAN QUESTION TIME

QUESTIONS:

1. Where was Celtic's first European game in season 2006/07 played?
2. And which player opened the scoring in that game?
3. Which two Celtic players returned to their own countries to play for Celtic in Europe last season?
4. And when Celtic reached the last 16 of the Champions League, which player returned to the country where he used to play his domestic football?
5. Who scored a Champions League penalty for the Bhoys at Celtic Park during that campaign?
6. And who was that penalty against?
7. Which Celtic youngster made his European debut in an away match – his first ever away game in any competition?
8. Who scored the goal that took Celtic into the Champions League last 16 for the first time ever?
9. And why was Artur Boruc a hero in the same game?
10. Last season Celtic celebrated the 40th Anniversary of which event?

(Answers on Pages 60/61)

Did you know... That over 700 players have played first-team games for Celtic and, at the end of last season, 99 had played one game and one game only?

EARNING PASS MARKS
...with Paul Hartley

PAUL HARTLEY SAYS:

"The most important lesson you can learn in football is to work hard. I have played with good individuals before, but some people do not work hard enough and do not make the most of their talents.

If you work hard your ability will shine through and it's about being the best that you possibly can be.

Fitness is also very important when you are playing in midfield and you should always try and eat the right food, particularly if you are playing a game that day.

The things that you try and do in a game will depend on what kind of midfielder you are.

For example, if you are an attacking midfielder you should always be looking to make runs beyond the strikers.

But no matter what kind of player you are, you should work on your control, because in midfield it helps if you are comfortable on the ball. Then during a game, you should make passes, try and see things early and time your runs into the box to get on the end of things. When I was growing up it was just normal to be out playing football every single day. For young kids today there are a lot of

CELTIC in the COMMUNITY

TRAINING TIPS
- Try to look for a simple pass to a team-mate.
- Try and use the inside of your foot to pass the ball, this will help you achieve the best accuracy.
- Relax when passing the ball, to keep good technique.
- Pass the ball then move into space.
- Don't always follow your pass.

TRAINING EXERCISES
Keep your score in this simple competition where you and a friend can play against each other.

- If you don't have access to markers or cones, use jackets or jumpers.
- Start on a marker 10 yards from your friend.
- Halfway between both of you, place two cones a yard apart, creating a 'GATE'.
- Pass the ball through the gate to your friend and in doing so you get one goal.
- The ball must go through the gate without touching the cones.
- If your friend passes the ball back through the gates the score is then 1-1.
- Play for one minute and at the end the person with the most points is the winner!

distractions out there like computer games and DVDs, but if you want to be a player you have to make sacrifices and work hard, even when you might not feel like it.

It's important to have the right attitude and be respectful, handle yourself in the right manner and treat people well. You should also work on every aspect of your game, even the things that you might not be particularly comfortable doing and you should try and take the time to work on different things like crossing, passing, heading and finishing. But to do that you have to be self-motivated. People can tell you to go out and work, but if you want to be a player it's important to practice, work hard and motivate yourself."

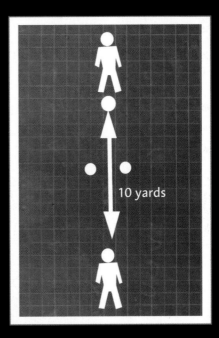

10 yards

CONTACT CELTIC IN THE COMMUNITY

For more information, or to book any Celtic in the Community course throughout Scotland:
Call the Hotline: 0871 226 1888 (Option 5)
Telephone: 0141 551 4321

120 YEARS OF CELTIC

1880s
1890s
1900s
1910s
1920s
1930s

THIS year 'The Grand Old Team' celebrates its 120th birthday, having grown from its beginnings as a charitable institution to become one of the world's most famous football clubs. Here we step back through the ages and look at the Celtic story, from the 1880s up to the present day.

1880s In November 1887 Celtic Football Club was founded by a Marist priest, Brother Walfrid, as a means of raising money for the poor in the East End of Glasgow. The fledgling team thumped Rangers 5-2 in their opening game in May 1888 in front of a crowd of over 2,000 and went on to reach the Scottish Cup final in their first season, where they were beaten 2-1 by Third Lanark.

1890s Celtic were one of the Scottish League's founder members in 1890/91, winning their opening game 5-0 against Hearts at Tynecastle. The following year they went on to win their first silverware, clinching the Scottish Cup with a 5-1 victory over Queen's Park. Then, in 1893, they clinched their first of four league titles that decade. By this point, the club had also made the switch from their first home just east of Janefield Cemetery to the 'Paradise' of Celtic Park.

1900s A new century kicked off with former player Willie Maley now settled as the club's manager. Maley's talented young side would win six league titles and four Scottish Cups as the new era began with a flair and attacking style that was praised throughout the football world. Celtic's six titles in a row between 1905-10 set a Scottish record that would not be matched until the 1970s. And just after the turn of the century – 1903 to be exact – Celtic changed their strip to the green and white hoops which would become famous throughout the world.

1910s With that first great Maley side beginning to age and its talismanic striker, Jimmy Quinn, struggling through injury, the manager began to build again with outstanding Patsy Gallagher at the heart of his plans. 'The Mighty Atom' would be central to Celtic's four title wins between 1914 and 1917, as the league continued under the shadow of the First World War- a conflict that claimed the lives of several Celts.

1920s - In 1922, James Edward McGrory made his debut in the Hoops, at first giving little hint of the greatness that was to come. In 445 first-team appearances, Jimmy McGrory would go on to score a remarkable 472 goals, with the Garngad-born striker ranked as Europe's top goalscorer in 1927 and 1936. The 'Roaring Twenties' also saw Celtic win a further two league titles as well as three Scottish Cups.

1930s This decade began with the tragic death of John Thomson on September 5, 1931 after an accidental collision in a game against Rangers. It was an event which marked the club forever, with the young goalkeeper still remembered as a Celtic great to this day. With Maley approaching his 70th birthday, his latest Celtic side now emerged. Spearheaded by McGrory, Jimmy Delaney and Willie Buchan and playing with outstanding flair and style, this side would win two league titles and three Scottish Cups as war once again threatened the world.

1940s The Second World War saw the league suspended for six years and even when play officially resumed in 1946, Celtic struggled to recover. With Maley having left the club in 1940 to be replaced with, first, Jimmy McStay and then, Jimmy McGrory, the immediate post-war seasons saw Celtic record some of the worst league results in the club's history, while the cup competitions also failed to provide a crumb of comfort for the supporters.

1950s

With a core of talented players now led by an inspirational captain, Jock Stein, Celtic emerged from the shadows in 1953/54, winning the league and Scottish Cup double in style before going on to beat Rangers 7-1 in the 1957 League Cup final. But this 'season in the sun' proved to be a false dawn and Celtic supporters continued to be frustrated as they saw their city rivals dominate the domestic scene even though their team had a string of talented individuals, such as Charlie Tully and Willie Fernie.

1960s

Celtic continued to struggle at the start of the Swinging '60s, even losing to Dunfermline in the 1961 Scottish Cup final. The Pars were managed by Jock Stein but just four years later he took over the reins at Paradise and kick-started the most successful period in the club's history. After winning the Scottish Cup in 1965, Celtic clinched the first of a record nine league titles in a row the following season. Then, in that celebrated 1966/67 season, Celtic won every single competition they entered, including the European Cup on May 25, 1967 when they defeated Inter Milan 2-1 in Lisbon to become the first British club to win the trophy.

1970s

The '70s kicked-off with Celtic narrowly missing out on another European triumph when they lost the European Cup final to Feyenoord at the San Siro stadium in Milan. But still the good times rolled on, with the likes of Billy McNeill, Bobby Lennox and Jimmy Johnstone at the heart of Scottish football's greatest team. Great young players, such as Kenny Dalglish and Danny McGrain, also continued to emerge at Celtic Park. Jock Stein was eventually succeeded as manager by his captain, McNeill, in 1978.

1980s

Four league titles, four Scottish Cups, a League Cup win and several memorable European Cup highlights saw Celtic continue to perform with all of their old cut and dash in this new decade. The centenary year of 1988 was the undoubted highlight of this era, with McNeill returning as manager to clinch the Double. But this success in many ways masked the problems that were to lie ahead in what was a painful, barren decade for the club.

1990s

After winning the Scottish Cup in 1989, Celtic fans had to wait six years for another trophy – when the Hoops won the same trophy against Airdrie. In the meantime, there had been big changes off the field, with Fergus McCann taking over the club in 1994 and saving Celtic from possible extinction. In 1997, Rangers equalled Celtic's nine-in-a-row, but Dutchman Wim Jansen arrived and helped Celtic 'stop the 10' the following season. However, he left at the end of the season and Celtic had to wait another three years before lifting the league trophy again.

2000s

On his arrival as manager, Martin O'Neill pledged to do his 'very best' to bring success to the club and this he did in style, ushering in an era of domestic dominance – starting with a 6-2 demolition of Rangers in August 2000 - and giving his team the confidence to succeed in the European arena. Celtic were to win three league titles and miss out on another two by goal difference and just one point during his five-year tenure. They also reached the 2003 UEFA Cup final in Seville. And this success has been continued by current boss, Gordon Strachan, whose side has won two championships, two cups and reached the last 16 of the UEFA Champions for the first time in the club's history.

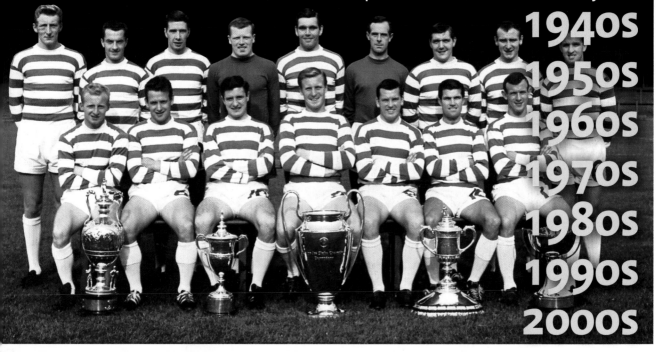

1940s
1950s
1960s
1970s
1980s
1990s
2000s

QUIZ ANSWERS

SPOT THE DIFFERENCE (Page 20)

SPL SEASON 2006/07 CHAMPIONSHIP QUIZ ANSWERS (Page 21)

01. Jan Vennegoor of Hesselink.
02. Shunsuke Nakamura
03. Rugby Park
04. Teddy Bjarnason
05. 84
06. Mark Brown
07. St Mirren 5-1
08. Jan Vennegoor of Hesselink
09. Hearts
10. 4-1 v Kilmarnock
11. 15
(Lee Naylor, Kenny Miller, Jan Vennegoor of Hesselink, Gary Caldwell, Jiri Jarosik, Thomas Gravesen, Steven Pressley, Evander Sno, Darren O'Dea, Paul Hartley, Derek Riordan, Jean-Joel Perrier-Doumbe, Teddy Bjarnason, Mark Brown, Cillian Sheridan)
12. 3

WORDSEARCH ANSWERS (Page 27)

01. Barrowfield
02. Portugal
03. Hoopy
04. Hampden
05. CelticView
06. Elvis
07. Motherwell
08. Gretna
09. Japan
10. Inverness

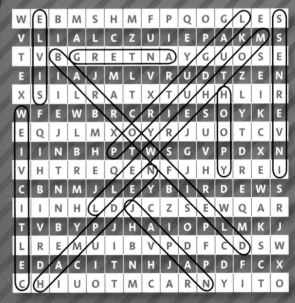

QUIZ ANSWERS
(Page 27)

01.   Scott Brown, with Hibs
02.   St Johnstone
03.   Manchester United
04.   Neil Lennon
05.   Three

MAZE (Page 26)

See opposite

GUESS WHO?
ANSWERS (Page 47)

01.   Artur Boruc
02.   Shunsuke Nakamura
03.   Kenny Miller
04.   Steven Pressley
05.   Evander Sno
06.   Jan Vennegoor of Hesselink

DOT TO DOT
ANSWER (Page 54)

Aiden McGeady

EURO QUIZ
ANSWERS (Page 55)

01.   Old Trafford.
02.   Jan Vennegoor of Hesselink.
03.   Lee Naylor in England (Man United)
      and Thomas Gravesen in Denmark (FC
      Copenhagen).
04.   Shunsuke Nakamura who used to play for
      Reggina in Italy.
05.   Kenny Miller.
06.   It came in the 1-0 win over FC
      Copenhagen.
07.   Darren O'Dea in Copenhagen, his previous
      two domestic starts were at Celtic Park.
08.   Shunsuke Nakamura against Manchester
      United.
09.   He saved a late penalty from Louis Saha.
10.   The Lisbon Lions winning the European
      Cup in 1967.

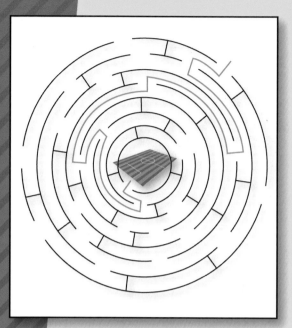